Do not cut ou

THE SHOPKEEPER WILL DO THIS FOR YOU

D6	D6	D6	D6	E6	E6	E6	E6
D5	D5	D5	D5	E5	E5	E5	E5
D4	D4	D4	D4	E4	E4	E4	E4
D3	D3	D3	D3	E3	E3	E3	E3
D2	D2	D2	D2	E2	E2	E2	E2
D1	D1	D1	D1	E1	E1	E1	E1

D1327934

'I say, I hope there'll be something to drink tonight. The wine outlook becomes increasingly desperate since France went. One didn't expect to have to fight the war on an occasional half-pint of bitter, and lucky if you find that.'

Anthony Powell, *The Soldier's Art*, 1966

RATION BOOK COOKERY

Recipes & History

by
Gill Corbishley

Edited by
Emily Allison

with a Foreword by
Loyd Grossman OBE

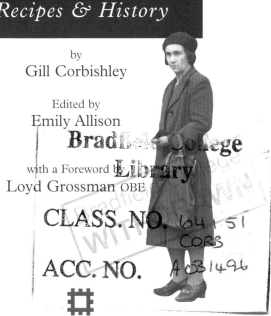

ENGLISH HERITAGE

Front cover: Huge queues formed themselves outside bakers' shops all over London on 20 July 1946 – the last day before the introduction of bread rationing

Endpapers: Rationing continued well after the war as shown by this book from the early 1950s

Published by English Heritage, 23 Savile Row, London W1S 2ET

Copyright © English Heritage and Gill Corbishley
First published 1985
Revised edition 2004
Reprinted 2009

ISBN 978 1 850748 71 7

Product code 50854

Project managed by Susan Kelleher, Publishing, English Heritage, Kemble Drive, Swindon SN2 2GZ
Designed by Pauline Hull
Brought to press by Andrew McLaren
Printed in England by Norwich Colour Print Ltd

Mixed Sources
Product group from well-managed forests and other controlled sources
www.fsc.org Cert no. TT-COC-002425
© 1996 Forest Stewardship Council
FSC

CONTENTS

FOREWORD

Would the pyramids have been built without the recently invented bread to efficiently feed the workforce? Food is a common denominator between us all, and a potent link with our ancestors, just as much as an ancient parish church or a listed house.

I am delighted to contribute a Foreword to English Heritage's series of historic cookery books, which neatly combine two of my passions – history and food. Most of us no longer have to catch or grow our own food before eating it, but the continuing daily need for sustenance still powerfully links us with our earliest forebears. We may not like the thought of Roman fish sauce made from fermented entrails (until we next add oyster sauce to a Chinese beef dish), but we can only sigh with recognition at a Jacobean wife's exhortation to 'let yor butter bee scalding hott in yor pan' before pouring in the beaten eggs for an omelette. The Roman penchant for dormice cooked in milk doesn't resonate with us now, but a dish of pears in red wine features at modern dinner parties just as it did in medieval times.

Food and cooking have inevitably changed down the centuries, as modern cookers have supplanted open hearths, and increased wealth and speedy transport have opened up modern tastes and palates to the widest range of ingredients and cuisines. But it's worth remembering that it was the Romans who gave us onions, sugar was an expensive luxury in the 16th century as was tea in the 17th, the tomato only became popular in Europe in the 19th century and even in the 1950s avocados and red peppers were still exotic foreign imports.

I urge you to experiment with the recipes in these books which cover over 2,000 years, and hope you enjoy, as I have, all that is sometimes strange and often familiar about the taste of times past.

Loyd Grossman OBE
Former Commissioner of English Heritage
Chairman of the Campaign for Museums

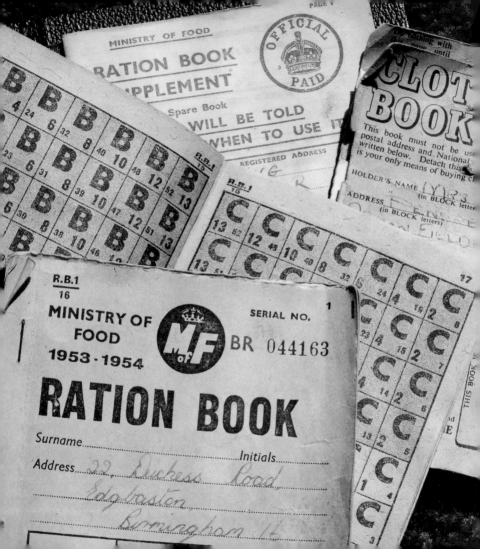

INTRODUCTION

The Second World War was an extraordinary period, and its impact on the social structure of Britain was immense. It changed the nation's diet and echoes of the privations and restrictions that people had to endure are still felt among those who lived through those turbulent times.

Supply ships bringing in Britain's imports were blockaded by the German navy and, at one time, one out of every four ships was sunk. The blockade, combined with the overriding necessity to use shipping for troops, threw the country back on its own

Wartime poster by Lieutenant Games encouraging the nation to produce home-grown food

WOMEN!

Farmers can't grow all your vegetables

YOU MUST GROW YOUR OWN

resources for food supplies. Suddenly, some of the staples of the British diet – meat, sugar and tea – were in drastically short supply. Imports of food between 1939 and 1945 were almost halved.

Before 1939, only one third of all the food eaten in Britain was actually grown there. The number of acres under cultivation had risen from 12,000,000 in 1939 to 18,000,000 in 1945, and the country was producing two-thirds of its food. The 'Kitchen Front' was essential in the battle against the enemy.

However, the impact on society was not confined to the war years. 'Austerity' and rationing dragged on until 1954. The habit of hoarding every stringy runner bean and giant marrow persists in many of those who lived through that traumatic time.

Opposite: A week's ration for one person

The limits and restrictions also had a positive effect. The health of the nation improved; people ate a more balanced diet and used their resources ingeniously. This recipe book includes some of the wartime favourites, as well as providing information on the particular effects of the war on food and cooking methods.

Many of the recipes are cooked in a moderate oven which is gas mark 4, 180°C, 350°F. They include clever combinations of flavours; the use of weeds instead of vegetables; and fooling the tastebuds with some interesting substitutes for luxury foodstuffs.

Left: A wedding breakfast during the war makes the best of limited resources

Opposite: A Liverpool demolition worker sucking a raw egg supplied from America under the Lease and Lend scheme

A CHRONOLOGY OF RATIONING

29 September 1939   National Register set up.
Identity cards issued

8 January 1940   Food rationing begins. Bacon, ham,
sugar and butter 'on the ration'

March 1940   Meat rationed

April 1940   Lord Woolton becomes Minister
of Food

July 1940   Tea, margarine, cooking fats
and cheese rationed

March 1941   Jam, marmalade, treacle
and syrup rationed

June 1941   Distribution of eggs
controlled

August 1941   Extra cheese rations
for manual workers

November 1941   Distribution of milk controlled

December 1941   National Dried Milk introduced. Points scheme for food.
Vitamin Welfare Scheme introduced

June 1942   American dried egg powder on sale

July 1942	Sweets rationed
December 1944	Extra tea allowance for 70-year-olds and over
January 1945	Whalemeat and snoek (fish like barracuda) available for sale
July 1946	Bread rationed

'OFF THE RATION'

July 1948	Bread
December 1948	Jam
October 1952	Tea
February 1953	Sweets
March 1953	Eggs
April 1953	Cream
September 1953	Sugar
May 1954	Butter, cheese, margarine and cooking fats
June 1954	Meat

NO MORE RATIONING!

Recipes

MOCK HARE SOUP

2 large potatoes
I leek
I carrot
I stick celery
¹/₂ turnip
15 g (¹/₂ oz) dripping
2 cloves
150 g (5 oz) course oatmeal
800 ml (1¹/₂ pt) stock or water
5 ml (I tsp) meat extract or cube
salt and pepper to taste

Chop vegetables, put in pan with dripping and fry thoroughly. Add oatmeal and cook until brown, stirring all the time to prevent burning. Add seasoning, cloves and stock and cook for ¹/₂ hour on a low heat. Sieve before serving, then add meat essence and reheat.

Good Eating: Suggestions for Wartime Dishes

'The battle on the Kitchen Front cannot be won without help from the Kitchen Garden.'

The Rt Hon Lord Woolton
Minister of Food

NETTLE SOUP

2 l (3¹/₂ pt) young nettles
2 blades of chives, or a little onion
90 ml (6 tbls) barley or oat flour
2 l (3/₂ pt) stock
salt and pepper

Clean the nettles and plunge them in boiling water. Boil for about 15 minutes. Pour off all the water and wash the nettles again in fresh running water. Cut them up finely with the chives or onion, sprinkle with flour, then frizzle in a little fat. Add the stock and then simmer for ³/₄ hour in a covered pan. Skim, season to taste, and serve.

A poached egg may be floated on the top.

The "Olio" Cookery Book

Nettles can be used instead of spinach. Rich in vitamins A and C, the young leaves are especially good and should be gathered early in spring. Wash well and allow a good panful as you would for spinach. Cook in their own juices with a very little water. When young and tender, they will take about 10 minutes to cook, after which they can be drained and the water put aside for soup. The nettles can be chopped finely and reheated in a little fat if you can spare it. Add seasoning, a grate of nutmeg and serve.

MOCK BEEF RISSOLES

100 g (4 oz) rice
425 ml (³/₄ pt) stock
2.5 ml (¹/₂ tsp) mustard
25 g (1 oz) grated horseradish
Marmite
salt and pepper

Boil the rice in vegetable stock for
³/₄ hour, add mustard and horseradish,
a little Marmite, salt and pepper, and
make into rissoles. Coat with oatmeal
or dip in egg and breadcrumbs, fry in
a basket in deep fat. Serve with
mashed potatoes and gravy.

The "Olio" Cookery Book

LORD WOOLTON PIE

450 g (1 lb) each of:
  diced potatoes, cauliflower,
  swedes and carrots
3 or 4 spring onions
5 ml (1 tsp) vegetable extract
5 ml (1 tsp) oatmeal
a little chopped parsley
225 g (½ lb) cooked, sliced potatoes
  or wholemeal pastry for topping

Place the diced vegetables, spring onions, vegetable extract and oatmeal into a saucepan, add just enough water to cover and cook for 10 minutes, stirring occasionally. Allow to cool. Put the mixture into a pie dish and sprinkle with parsley. Cover with the crust of potatoes or wholemeal pastry. Bake in a moderate oven until the topping is nicely brown and serve hot with gravy.

Government Recipes

MEALIE PUDDING ('DONKEY')

1 large onion or 2 leeks
275 ml (½ pt) medium oatmeal
50 g (2 oz) chopped suet
salt and pepper
575 ml (1 pt) cold water

Chop the onion or leeks finely and blend well with the oatmeal, suet, salt and pepper. Mix with a pint of cold water to make a soft dough. Put into a greased basin leaving plenty of room for it to swell. Steam for 3 hours. Turn out and serve hot or cold.

Food Facts

In the 1930s, an American company called Hormel developed a canned luncheon meat which they named Hormel Spiced Ham. Worried about competition, they decided they would make their product more marketable by changing its name. So they launched a competition offering $100 for the best idea. As a result, Spam was born. Launched in 1937, 'the Miracle Meat', was promoted widely and even given its own jingle:

Spam, Spam, Spam, Spam,
Hormel's new miracle meat in a can,
Tastes fine, saves time,
If you want something grand,
Ask for Spam!

During the Second World War sales boomed, and this versatile luncheon meat appeared on the table at breakfast, lunch and tea – fried, battered or just on its own.

VEGETABLE AND OATMEAL GOULASH

450 g (1 lb) mixed root
  vegetables
knob of dripping
50 g (2 oz) course or medium
  oatmeal
sprinkling of paprika
chopped parsley and herbs to
  flavour
salt and pepper to taste
5 ml (1 tsp) meat extract or
  stock cube
vegetable stock

Prepare and dice the vegetables. Fry in dripping until slightly cooked; add oatmeal and stir over fire until fat is absorbed. Season with paprika, herbs, salt and pepper and add meat extract. Cover with vegetable stock and simmer gently for 1 hour.

A little corned beef, cooked meat or fish may be added at the last minute.

Good Eating: Suggestions for Wartime Dishes

HASHED MEAT

Stew any bones and trimmings of meat in cold gravy, stock or water, adding a little finely chopped carrot. Strain, thicken, put in any other sliced meat (over or cut into little squares) you have left; let it get hot. Serve with toast around the meat and gravy poured over.

The "Olio" Cookery Book

BOSTON BAKE

425 ml (³/₄ pt) small white beans
75 g (3 oz) diced bacon
450 g (1 lb) sliced carrots
5 ml (1 tsp) dry mustard
15 ml (1 tbls) golden syrup

Soak the beans in cold water for 24 hours. Put these into a stew jar with most of the bacon and carrots. Mix the dry mustard and golden syrup with enough hot water to make 275 ml (¹/₂ pt) liquid. Pour over beans and add enough water to cover. Put on lid and bake in a moderate oven for 2–2¹/₂ hours. In the last ¹/₂ hour of cooking, remove the lid and sprinkle with the remaining bacon to brown off.

Government Recipes

MOCK GOOSE

150 g (6 oz) split red lentils
275 ml (¹/₂ pt) water
15 ml (1 tbls) lemon juice
salt and pepper

For the 'stuffing':
1 large onion, chopped
50 g (2 oz) wholemeal fresh breadcrumbs
15 ml (1 tbls) fresh sage, chopped

Cook the lentils in the water until all the water has been absorbed. Add lemon juice and season. Then make the 'stuffing'. Sauté the onion in a little water or vegetable stock for 10 minutes. Drain, then add to the breadcrumbs. Mix in the chopped sage and mix well. Put half the lentil mixture into a non-stick ovenproof dish, spread the 'stuffing' on top, then top off with the remaining lentils. Put in a moderate oven until the top is crisp and golden.

'Not mustard, Bobbums, though well you might have thought so, for what you need with all this American tinned stuff, though it is wonderful of them to lease-lend us all their Spam and what not, is mustard.'

Angela Thirkell,
Growing Up, 1945

MOCK CRAB

1 piece of ray or skate
1 yolk of hard-boiled egg
   (or 1 dried egg)
salt, pepper and mustard
anchovy (or essence)
10 ml (2 tsp) cream
10 ml (2 tsp) salad oil
5 ml (1 tsp) vinegar

To serve:
crab shell
lettuce leaves

Boil the fish, flake whilst hot, then let it cool. Take the yolk (or dried egg), season with salt, pepper, mustard and anchovy (or essence). Mix in a little cream, salad oil and vinegar to moisten, then pour over the fish. Serve in a crab shell with lettuce leaves.

The "Olio" Cookery Book

MOCK FISH CAKES

150 g (5 oz) boiled potatoes or rice
150 g (5 oz) boiled beans
little lemon juice
10 ml (2 tsp) anchovy sauce or bloater paste
cayenne
sprinkle of flour to bind

Mix all the ingredients together and beat up well. Make the mixture into little flat cakes, and fry or bake until golden brown. Serve with salad.

The "Olio" Cookery Book

SARDINE FRITTERS

1 tin sardines

For batter:
45 ml (3 tbls) flour
salt and pepper
1 egg
milk

Leave the sardines to drain from the oil. Put the flour in a basin with the salt and pepper. Put the yolk of the egg in a well in the centre and add enough milk to form a smooth batter. Beat up the white of the egg and stir in lightly. Place a sardine on a tablespoon and dip the spoon in the batter to coat the fish. Dry fry in a lightly greased frying pan, turning the fritters once. Drain on paper and decorate with parsley and slices of lemon.

War Time Cookery Book

'Mrs George Pollett, wife of the Sheep's Head, was renowned far and wide for her fried fish and her steak and kidney puddings, which, alas, were now but beautiful memories. Yet even under the peculiar arrangements for fish known as zoning, a word accepted placidly by the population of England and with their genius for misinterpretation at once reduced to a synonym of total disappearance, Mrs Pollett managed to do wonders with an occasional bit of frozen cod, and her meat ration always went twice as far as anyone else's.'

Angela Thirkell, *Growing Up*, 1945

BAKED COD WITH PARSNIP BALLS AND PIQUANT SAUCE

900 g (2 lb) parsnips
salt and pepper
browned crumbs
450 g (1 lb) soaked salt cod
60 ml (4 tbls) dripping

For the sauce:
15 g (¹/₂ oz) margarine
30 ml (2 tbls) flour
275 ml (¹/₂ pt) vegetable stock
salt, pepper and mustard
15 ml (1 tbls) vinegar

Cook the parsnips until quite soft. Drain and mash well with seasonings. Form into balls and coat in browned crumbs. Skin and bone the fish, place in a baking tin and spread with dripping. Bake in a hot oven for 5 minutes, then add parsnip balls and bake together for 20 minutes.

For the sauce:
Melt the margarine, add flour and cook for 3 minutes. Add the stock gradually, stirring well, and cook for another 5 minutes. Season and stir in the vinegar. Serve with the fish in the centre of the dish, the parsnip balls around it and the sauce over the fish.

Government Recipes

29

Although commercial advertising was actually restricted during the war because of lack of space in magazines and scarcity of paper for printing – not to mention a scarcity of goods – Government advertisements are one of the richest sources of evidence. The Government was able to capitalise on people's good will.

The methods of war may be horrible to the verge of idiocy. But war has this redeeming sanity, that its purpose is clear and the methods that it uses are logically directed towards the achievement of that purpose. It is the feeling of common and intelligible purpose, far more than any heroics, that reconciles people to war. The chaos of production for private and conflicting interests goes. The ploughman in the fields, the sailor and fisherman are not just getting something to be sold, or thrown away if the price offered is too low; they are supplying the needs of the people.'

J R Marrack,
Food and Planning, 1942

Feeding 45 Millions –
UNLOADING

EGG AND RICE LOAF

75 g (3 oz) rice
575 ml (1 pt) vegetable boilings
   (or stock)
3 reconstituted dried eggs
15 ml (1 tbls) chopped parsley
15 ml (1 tbls) chopped onion
15 ml (1 tbls) tomato sauce
salt and pepper

To serve:
parsley sauce or tomato sauce

Put the rice into a saucepan with the stock, cover and cook gently until the rice is tender and all the stock is absorbed. Reconstitute the eggs and add them to the rice with the parsley, onion, tomato sauce and seasoning. Turn into a greased pudding basin, or a cake tin, and steam or bake in a moderate oven until the mixture is set. This should take about 1 hour. Turn out and serve with parsley or tomato sauce.

Government Recipes

RULES FOR USING DRIED EGG

1. Store in a cool, dry place and replace the lid of the tin after use.

2. To turn a dried egg into a fresh one, mix one level tablespoon of the powder with two tablespoons of water – this mixture equals one fresh egg.

3. Now treat the egg as you would a fresh one. Don't make up more egg than necessary for the dish you are making. Beat as usual before adding to other ingredients.

Government Recipes

VITALITY MOULD

1.4 kg (3 lbs) spinach
25g (1 oz) margarine
2 beaten eggs
pinch of mixed herbs
salt and pepper
a little allspice
115 ml (7 tbls) fine white
breadcrumbs

To serve:
white sauce

Wash the spinach thoroughly in several changes of water. Put into a large saucepan with a very little salt and cook slowly without the addition of any extra water until it is quite tender. Rub through a sieve. Melt the margarine in a saucepan and stir in the sieved spinach. Season. Add the herbs, breadcrumbs and beaten egg. Blend well and put into a well-greased basin. Cover with greased paper and steam for about 30–45 minutes until the mixture is set and firm Serve with white sauce.

War Time Cookery Book

POTATO SCONES

225 g ('/2 lb) mashed potato
225 g ('/2 lb) flour
pinch of salt
2.5 ml ('/2 tsp) baking powder
milk
15 ml (1 tbls) dripping

Mix the potato, flour, salt and baking powder together with enough milk to make a stiff paste. Roll out about 5 mm ('/4 in) thick. Fry the first cake in a little dripping, the others will do without. Butter, and serve hot, in a pile.

The "Olio" Cookery Book

MIDDLETON MEDLEY

Beat some mashed potato with a little milk, including a little egg if possible. Pipe with forcing bag, or mould with a fork, into little nest shapes. Bake these in a hot oven for 15 minutes until lightly browned. Fill with one of the following:

1. Diced cooked carrots and turnips, with a sprinkling of finely chopped parsley.

2. Small cooked sprouts sprinkled with finely grated cheese or ground mixed nuts. Substitute spinach when in season.

Food Facts

'Somebody ought to write a song in praise of the potato. It is cheap. It is nourishing. It is an Energy Food and a Protective Food. It can be cooked in an endless variety of interesting ways. The potato does an all-round wartime job. It contains the valuable Vitamin C, the vitamin we miss when food is scarce. It can save us flour and fat when we use it in making cakes, scones, puddings and pastries. And medical advice encourages us each to eat 1 lb of potatoes every day.'

Food Facts

RED CABBAGE CASSEROLE

1 small red cabbage
a small onion or a little minced spring onion
225 g (8 oz) apples
25 g (1 oz) dripping
10 ml (2 tsp) flour
salt and pepper
275 ml (¹/₂ pt) water or stock
¹/₂ bay leaf
vinegar

Wash and halve the cabbage, remove the centre tough stalk and shred or slice the leaves into thin pieces. Chop the onion finely and peel and quarter the apples. Place cabbage, onion and apples into the melted dripping in a casserole and sauté for a few minutes. Stir in flour, season and then add the water or stock. Add the bay leaf, then simmer gently until the cabbage is tender, adding vinegar to taste. This dish is excellent served with sausages or, to make a meal in itself, add a little chopped bacon to the cabbage just before serving.

Food Facts

'We must grow our own onions. We can no longer import ninety per cent of them, as we did before the war.'

The Rt Hon Lord Woolton, Minister of Food

TO PRESERVE BEANS IN SALT

Allow 450 g (1 lb) salt for every 1.4 kg (3 lbs) beans

The beans must be young, fresh and tender. Do not wash unless necessary. If washed, dry before slicing. Cut them up (if small they may be left whole). Place a good layer of salt in a stoneware jar and on the salt add a layer of beans. Continue to fill up the jar with alternate layers, pressing beans well down and always with a top layer of salt. Cover and leave for a few days. The beans will shrink and the jar may then be filled up with more beans and salt, but take care that the final layer of salt completely covers the beans. Cover the jar securely with the lid or several layers of paper; if using cork, paint over with melted paraffin wax. If the jar is stored in a room with a stone floor, place on a piece of wood.

To use the beans:

Remove the salt and soak in two or three lots of cold water for 12 hours at least. Cook in boiling water until tender.

Good Fare

A clear plate means A clear conscience

Don't take more than you can eat

BEETROOT AND CELERY

5–6 stalks of celery
2–3 cooked beetroots
(depending on size)
a little margarine or dripping
lemon juice
a little chopped parsley
salt and pepper

Cook the celery in boiling salted water, drain well. Chop into conveniently sized pieces. Cut the beetroot into similarly sized pieces and place in a pan together with the celery. Add the margarine or dripping, lemon juice, chopped parsley and seasoning and stir together over a gentle heat until thoroughly hot.

War Time Cookery Book

CARROT ROLL

2 large carrots
salt and pepper
5 ml (1 tsp) vegetable extract
10 ml (2 tsps) fine oatmeal, toasted
cold cooked mashed potato

Grate the carrots coarsely and cook for 10 minutes in a very little water. Season well and add the vegetable extract and toasted oatmeal. Boil for 5 minutes, stirring to thicken. Cool. At this stage the mixture will be quite stiff. Have some cold mashed potato ready, dust the pastry board with flour and roll out into an oblong shape. Place the carrot filling in the centre, then fold over and shape into a roll. Dot with a few shavings of fat and bake in a moderately hot oven until nicely browned. Serve with well seasoned brown gravy.

Food Facts

CURRIED CARROTS

450 g (1 lb) carrots
25 g (1 oz) margarine or
dripping
1 chopped onion
7.5 ml (1½ tsp) curry powder
15 ml (1 tbls) flour
275 ml (½ pt) stock or water
salt and pepper

Trim carrots and boil in the usual way. For the curry sauce: melt the fat in a saucepan, add the onion and fry for a few minutes. Add the curry powder and flour and fry for a few more minutes, stirring occasionally. Then stir in the stock or water, bring to the boil and season to taste. Simmer gently for about 30 minutes. Add the cooked carrots to the sauce and cook for a further 20–30 minutes. Serve with a garnish of cooked rice.

STEWED CHESTNUTS

450 g (1 lb) chestnuts
275 ml (¹/₂ pt) boiling water
5 ml (1 tsp) flour
15 g (1¹/₂ oz) butter or
**   margarine**
15 ml (1 tbls) milk
salt and pepper

Shell the nuts and put into boiling water. Remove skins, thicken water with the flour and boil in this until tender (about 1¹/₂ hours). Strain off water, mash as you would turnips with the butter, milk, salt and pepper. Serve with meat.

The "Olio" Cookery Book

PASSION DOCK PUDDING

Boil tender dock leaves with green onions or spring onions (or, if not available, then with ordinary onions). When cooked add a handful of oatmeal or wheatmeal, one beaten egg and 5 ml (1 tsp) of butter or margarine. Simmer for ¹/₂ hour.

The nutritive value of this square meal recipe would be increased by the inclusion of some yeast extract.

Government Recipes

PEANUT SALAD

15 ml (1 tbls) peanut butter
30 ml (2 tbls) mashed potato
15 ml (1 tbls) chopped onion
   (or 30 ml (2 tbls) chives)
salt and pepper
sliced beetroot or tomato
lettuce leaves
salad dressing
a little grated cheese or
   chopped ham

Put peanut butter, potato, onion and seasoning in a bowl. Beat well together, then form into small balls. Mount each on a slice of beetroot or tomato. Arrange lettuce leaves in a bowl and place mounted peanut balls on them. Serve the salad dressing separately and a dish of grated cheese or thinly sliced chopped ham.

Good Eating: Suggestions for Wartime Dishes

SUNSET SALAD

Save your orange peel for this, and when you have some hot mashed potato mix some grated orange rind into it. Quickly beat it in until thoroughly blended when the mixture will take on a pretty pinky-orange colour. Whip creamy with a little vinaigrette or mock-mayonnaise and include a little grated or finely chopped celery or spring onion. Pile on to a bed of grated cabbage or broken lettuce and decorate with a few sprigs of heart celery or centre green tufts. A few sprigs of watercress make an attractive contrast of colour.

Food Facts

Opposite: A wartime poster encouraging people to put up with privations

BETTER POT-LUCK

with
Churchill
today

THAN HUMBLE PIE

under
Hitler
tomorrow

DON'T WASTE FOOD!

EGGLESS MAYONNAISE

1 small baked potato
5 ml (1 tsp) mustard
salt
a little vinegar
150 ml (¼ pt) salad oil

Peel and mash the potato, stir in the mustard and salt, then add the vinegar gradually, beating well. Last of all, beat in the salad oil slowly, mixing well.

Food Facts

EGGLESS SALAD DRESSING

45 ml (3 tbls) evaporated milk
30 ml (2 tbls) olive oil
2.5 ml (½ tsp) salt
pepper
a little mustard
15 ml (1 tbls) lemon juice
10 ml (2 tsp) vinegar

Whip the evaporated milk until frothy. Add the oil very slowly, beating hard all the time. Continue to beat until the sauce thickens. Add the seasonings, mustard, lemon juice and vinegar and blend thoroughly.

War Time Cookery Book

'It was the habit of Mavis and her friends to have meals all day; they barely paused between breakfast, morning coffee, early lunch, afternoon coffee, afternoon tea, late tea, supper and bedtime snacks... It was the war that had done this to them, turning life into one continuous quest for food – food to take home, food to consume in shops, food no longer a means but life's great end. Rations, dictated by coupons, had to be bought; to leave them unbought would be a sinful waste; bacons, fats, sweets, biscuits, everything in tins, were week by week absorbed; people grew in stature and in weight, and clothes were let out.

Rose Macauley, *The World My Wilderness*, 1950

RASPBERRY SNOW

575 ml (1 pt) milk
150 ml (¹/₄ pint) water
50 g (2 oz) sago
50 g (2 oz) sugar
30 ml (2 tbls) raspberry jam
a little lemon juice
a little red food colouring
  (optional)

Boil the milk and water, sprinkle in the sago and cook thoroughly. Add the sugar. Allow to cool and beat up with the raspberry jam and lemon juice. Add a little red food colouring if liked. Serve alone or with fruit.

War Time Cookery Book

PORTMAN PUDDING

50 g (2 oz) fat
30 ml (2 tbls) sugar
100 g (4 oz) grated raw carrot
100 g (4 oz) grated raw potato
165 g (6 oz) flour
pinch of salt
5 ml (1 tsp) mixed spice
5 ml (1 tsp) bicarbonate of soda
115 ml (7 tbls) sultanas and
  raisins

Cream fat and sugar, add carrot, potato, flour, salt, spice and soda. Mix well together. Add fruit. Add water if necessary to make a stiff dropping consistency. Steam for at least 2 hours. A sweet that needs little sugar!

Government Recipes

EGGLESS PANCAKES

30 ml (2 tbls) flour
pinch each of salt and sugar
milk and water to bind
lard or dripping

To serve:
jam, treacle, orange or lemon
juice

Mix the flour, salt and sugar with some milk and water to make a thick batter. Heat the lard or dripping until smoking hot. Drop in about 15 ml (1 tbls) of the mixture and cook until brown. Turn the pancake over and brown the other side. Eat with jam, treacle, orange or lemon juice.

The "Olio" Cookery Book

SAUCER PUDDING

15 ml (1 tbls) sugar
50 g (2 oz) butter
75 g (3 oz) flour
2.5 ml (1/2 tsp) baking powder
1 dried egg
a little milk
some jam for a filling

Mix all the ingredients together as you would a cake. Divide into two and place each of them onto a separate, greased saucer. Bake for about 15 minutes. Cool, add jam to one of the cakes and place the other on top of it.

The "Olio" Cookery Book

NORFOLK PUDDING

75 g (3 oz) rice
575 ml (1 pt) milk
50 g (2 oz) suet
25 g (1 oz) candied peel
25 g (1 oz) currants
50 g (2 oz) sultanas
40 g (1 1/2 oz) sugar
a little grated nutmeg
a pinch of salt

Wash the rice well and cook in the milk, using a double saucepan if one is available. Chop the suet and peel finely, add to the rice with the currants and sultanas. Add the sugar, nutmeg and salt, and beat together thoroughly. Put into a well-greased pie-dish and bake in a slow oven for a few minutes.

War Time Cookery Book

POTATO CHEESECAKES

75 g (3 oz) sugar
75 g (3 oz) butter
1 lemon
1 dried egg
1 large boiled potato
pastry

Dissolve the sugar in a pan with the butter, the grated rind of half a lemon, some lemon juice and the beaten egg. Mash the potato and add to the mixture (make sure it's lump-free!). Line some patty pans with pastry, fill them with the mixture and bake in a moderate oven for about 1/2 hour, or until golden brown.

The "Olio" Cookery Book

FOLKESTONE CHEESECAKES

275 ml (¹/₂ pt) milk
50 g (2 oz) sugar
40 g (1¹/₂ oz) ground rice
1 dried egg
pinch of salt
**bay leaf or piece of lemon or
    orange rind**
**enough pastry to cover a
    medium-sized flat plate**
some dry bread crusts
jam (optional)

Mix the milk, sugar and rice together; beat the egg with a pinch of salt and stir into the mixture. Add a bay leaf or a piece of lemon or orange rind and cook until it boils. Remove the leaf or rind and simmer for about 10 minutes. Line a flat plate with pastry. Cover with the dry bread crusts, blind bake, remove crusts, and cover pastry with the milk mixture. Bake until nicely browned. A layer of jam on the pastry before adding the milk mixture is an improvement.

The "Olio" Cookery Book

MOCK CLOTTED CREAM
(dried milk method)

50 g (2 oz) margarine
5 ml (1 tsp) sugar
15 ml (1 tbls) dried milk
few drops vanilla essence

Beat margarine and sugar together. By degrees, add the dried milk. Flavour with vanilla and beat until very smooth.

Good Eating: Suggestions for Wartime Dishes

Opposite: Ticking off the jam ration boxes at a local village shop

GINGER CREAM

1 packet of orange jelly
1 small tin evaporated milk
50 g (2 oz) preserved ginger
water (see jelly packet for
** quantity)**

Dissolve the jelly in sufficient water and add a little ginger syrup from the jar to make up to 425 ml (³/₄ pint). Add the evaporated milk and the ginger chopped into small pieces when almost set. Stir slightly in order to distribute the ginger evenly. Turn into a wetted mould. Stand in a cool place to set.

War Time Cookery Book

BAKED OR BOILED CUSTARD

15 ml (1 tbls) sugar
3 reconstituted eggs
575 ml (1 pt) milk (warmed)
few drops of vanilla essence
small piece of margarine
grate of nutmeg

Stir sugar into the eggs, then add warm milk and vanilla. Pour into a fireproof dish, adding margarine flaked in tiny pieces and nutmeg on top. Stand dish in a moderate oven in a tin of hot water to prevent curdling. Stir custard before it sets so that the margarine is well mixed with other ingredients.

Good Eating: Suggestions for Wartime Dishes

APRICOT UPSIDE-DOWN PUDDING

50 g (2 oz) dried apricots
75 g (3 oz) suet
225 g (8 oz) flour
pinch of salt
5 ml (1 tsp) baking powder
75 g (3 oz) sugar
2.5 ml ('/2 tsp) cinnamon
little milk for mixing

Soak the apricots overnight if possible.
Chop the suet finely and mix with
the flour, salt, baking powder, sugar
and cinnamon. Grease a cake tin, and
decorate the bottom with apricots.
Chop the remaining fruit and add to
the flour mixture. Mix with the milk.
Place in the cake tin, on top of the
apricots, cover with greased paper and
steam for 2 hours. Turn out onto a
cooling rack and serve with custard.

War Time Cookery Book

RHUBARB JAM

Cut rhubarb into short lengths. Put
225 g (8 oz) of sugar to each 450 g
(1 lb) of rhubarb. Let it stand for
24 hours, then boil for 15 minutes
without adding any water. Flavour with
either lemon rind or root ginger.

The "Olio" Cookery Book

RHUBARB BREAD PUDDING

225 g (8 oz) stale bread
jam for spreading
6 sticks of rhubarb
150 ml (¹/₄ pt) water
10 ml (2 tsps) custard powder
275 ml (¹/₂ pt) milk and water

Cut the bread into neat thick slices. Spread each one with jam. Cut the sticks of rhubarb into 25 mm (1 inch) pieces and stew these in a pan with a little water until almost tender. Strain the fruit, retaining the liquid, and lay the pieces in the bottom of a pie-dish. Cover the fruit with a layer of bread and jam slices, add another layer of fruit, then another layer of bread. Pour the rhubarb liquid (which should still be hot) over the fruit and bread and leave to soak for ¹/₂ hour. Mix the custard powder smoothly with a little milk and make it up to 275 ml (¹/₂ pt) with hot milk and water. Pour the uncooked custard into the pie-dish and bake in a moderate oven for 20 minutes. Serve hot or cold.

Food Facts

TO MAKE STALE BREAD LIKE NEW

Dip the loaf in and out of cold water or milk, quickly. Put in a greased tin, or greased paper bag. Bake in a moderate oven until crisp and it will eat like new! NB: Do not let it get too wet.

The "Olio" Cookery Book

CAKE OR PUDDING

**350 g (12 oz) hot, mashed
  potatoes**
flour to bind
**100–165 g (4–6 oz) dripping,
  lard, suet or mixture**
**75 g (3 oz) sultanas or similar
  dried fruit**
50 g (2 oz) sugar
pinch of salt
nutmeg

Mix the potatoes with a little flour to bind. Work in the fat, sultanas, sugar, salt and nutmeg. Add more flour to make a fairly stiff dough.

Put the mixture in a greased shallow tin and bake in a slow oven until crisp and brown. Serve hot for tea or with custard as a luncheon sweet.

Good Eating: Suggestions for Wartime Dishes

WAR AND PEACE CHRISTMAS PUDDING

This pudding was made in Canada during the First World War. It makes a good wartime Christmas pudding.

225 g (8 oz) flour
225 g (8 oz) breadcrumbs
100 g (4 oz) suet
100 g (4 oz) dried fruit
5 ml (1 tsp) mixed spice
225 g (8 oz) grated raw potato
225 g (8 oz) grated raw carrot
5 ml (1 tsp) bicarbonate of soda

Mix all the ingredients together and turn into a well-greased pudding bowl. The bowl should not be more than two-thirds full. Boil or steam for at least 2 hours.

Food Facts

BIBLE CAKE

This puzzling recipe uses quotations from the Bible as the key to the ingredients. Look up the references and work out what's required. It won't taste too good if you get it wrong!

1. **225 g ('/₂ lb) Judges V, verse 25 (last clause)**
2. **225 g ('/₂ lb) Jeremiah VI, 20**
3. **15 ml (1 tbls) I Samuel XIV, 25**
4. **3 of Jeremiah XVII, 11**
5. **225 g ('/₂ lb) I Samuel XXX, 12**
6. **225 g ('/₂ lb) Nahum III, 12 (chopped)**
7. **50 g (2 oz) Numbers XVII, 8 (blanched and chopped)**
8. **450 g (1 lb) I Kings IV, 22**
9. **Season to taste with II Chronicles IX, 9**
10. **a pinch of Leviticus II, 13**
11. **5 ml (1 tsp) Amos IV, 5**
12. **45 ml (3 tbls) Judges IV, 19**

(**HINT:** 'leaven' means 'baking powder' and you may need to add some Exodus III, 14 to moisten mixture)

Beat 1, 2 and 3 to a cream; add 4, one at a time, still beating; then 5, 6 and 7, and beat again. Add 8, 9, 10 and 11 having previously mixed them, and lastly 12. Bake in a slow oven for 1'/₂ hours.

The "Olio" Cookery Book

PINK LAYER PARTY CAKE

75 g (3 oz) sugar
50 g (2 oz) margarine
150 g (5 oz) self-raising flour
150 g (5 oz) pink blancmange or
    pudding powder
2 dried eggs reconstituted in
    milk
jam

Icing**:**
30 ml (2 tbls) sugar
30 ml (2 tbls) water
small piece margarine
pink blancmange powder

Beat the sugar and margarine together. Mix the flour and blancmange powder together. Add the egg and flour alternately to the sugar mixture. Beat together well. Put the mixture into two greased sandwich tins and bake in a moderate oven for 20 minutes. When cold, spread with a layer of jam and stick the two cakes together. To ice, boil the sugar, water and margarine together; allow to cool and mix in enough pink blancmange powder to make the icing of the right colour and consistency.

Good Eating: Suggestions for Wartime Dishes

CRUNCHIES

100 g (4 oz) margarine, lard or
  clarified dripping
50 g (2 oz) sugar
50 g (2 oz) syrup
150 g (5 oz) plain flour
100 g (4 oz) medium oatmeal
5 ml (1 tsp) baking powder
vanilla flavouring

Cream together the fat, sugar and
syrup. Add flour, oatmeal, baking
powder and a few drops of vanilla.
Knead until the mixture binds. Roll out
about 5 mm (¼ in) thick, cut into
rounds or fingers. Bake in a moderate
oven until golden brown for about 20
minutes. These biscuits keep well
stored in air-tight tins.

Good Eating: Suggestions for Wartime Dishes

MOCK MARZIPAN

225 g (8 oz) haricot beans
60 ml (4 tbls) sugar
30 ml (2 tbls) ground rice
15 ml (1 tbls) margarine
5 ml (1 tsp) almond essence

Soak the beans for 24 hours, then
cook until tender in fresh, unsalted
water. Put them on a tin in a warm
oven to get dry and floury. Rub them
through a sieve. Beat the sugar into
the bean purée, add the ground rice,
warmed margarine and, finally, the
flavouring. Beat until smooth. Any
flavouring or colouring matter may be
added.

Government Recipes

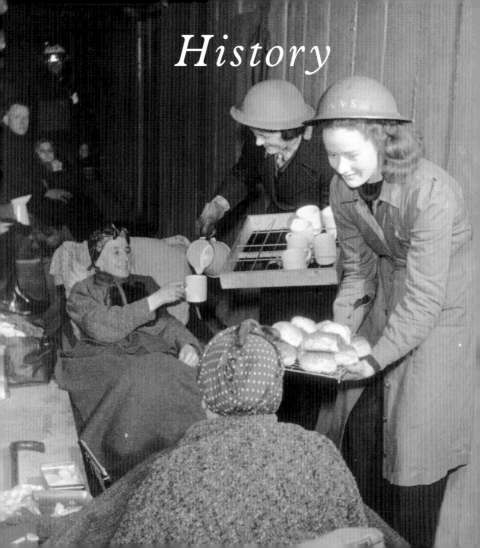

ADMINISTRATION

The government set up the Food (Defence Plans) Department as early as November 1936. The task of feeding the fighting forces so that they stayed strong and healthy almost pales into insignificance when compared with the enormous problem of feeding the back-up workers in factories, on the land and in offices – not to mention the population at large. On 29 September 1939 the National Register was set up and everybody was supplied with an identity card. By January 1940 ration books had been issued and butter, bacon and sugar were 'on the ration'. In March of that year meat was first rationed and in May, a 'Limitation of Supply Order' restricted the production of non-essential consumer goods.

Rationing seems to have worked well in most of the country through the war.

Opposite: Defying the Blitz to bring tea and buns to the occupants of a trench shelter

Right: Her Royal Highness Princess Elizabeth's ration book

Although there was a 'black market' in London and other towns, it does not seem to have been as damaging as those in Germany and the occupied countries. Perhaps the main responsibility for the success should be attributed to the newly-created Ministry of Food and, especially to the Minister, Lord Woolton.

The Ministry of Food set up Advice Bureaus to help people adapt to the restrictions

The Ministry employed cooks, such as Marguerite Patten, to staff their advice centres in places like school kitchens and the foyer in Harrods. The public was bombarded with help and guidance, via Food Facts in magazines, Food Flashes at the cinema and the daily five-minute radio programme Kitchen Front, which was on every morning after the eight o'clock news. Who could forget, or fail to respond to, jingles like:

'Those who have the will to win
Cook potatoes in their skin
Knowing that the sight of peelings
Deeply hurts Lord Woolton's feelings.'

The government's publicity efforts were not simply confined to helping the public to use the sorts of food easily available. In order for that extra 6,000,000 acres to

"I've Found the Meat Cards!"

DIG FOR VICTORY

For their sake -
GROW YOUR OWN VEGETABLES

produce food, campaigns such as 'Dig for Victory', and drives to recruit land girls and to persuade not only 'the big man with the plough' but 'the little man with the spade' to turn every spare yard of earth over to the production of food were constantly underway. Those with suitable gardens were encouraged to keep chickens and a pig, and could discover how to cook every bit of them in booklets like *Good Housekeeping's 100 Recipes for Unrationed Meat Dishes*.

These efforts were not unsuccessful. Allotments flourished in many a London park, like Hampstead Heath – fertile, convenient for large numbers of householders but unfortunately not numerous enough to counteract completely the deficiencies in everyone's diet.

Green vegetables, fruit and eggs from home-range hens were still not available for many people during the war years. A limiting factor for many would-be poultry farmers was the fact that grain for chicken food was as scarce as for bread manufacture.

'Points' were introduced into food ration books on 1 December 1941. They had been necessary for clothes since June; now tinned foods, which had previously been unrationed, could only be bought if one had both enough money and enough points left from the sixteen allocated to each person every month, to afford them. Naturally, the scarcer and more nutritious (or more appetising) food cost more points.

Opposite: Boys living in the blitzed East End of London create a garden among the rubble

Right: The Albert Memorial in the centre of London is set in a row of allotments as every available space is dug up for food production

ADJUSTMENT

Violet Plimmer, author of *Food Values in War Time* published in 1941, begins her book: 'The joys of the rationing system can only be fully appreciated by those who had to cater for a family during the last war.' She maintains that millions of hours were spent queuing for food during the First World War and that 'the biggest pusher or the owner of the swankiest fur coat got served first'. Her pious hope that rationing would eliminate queuing was not realised in the next few years. For many people, the only way to get hold of the 'optional extras' such as offal or onions was to join a queue. Price regulation and ration books did their best to ensure that much of the staple food which was available was distributed fairly but scarce supplies meant that the customer who wanted the best meat and the freshest vegetables was still forced to queue.

But how to find substitutes for the variety of ordinary foods like onions, eggs, cheese, bananas, tomatoes, sausages, meat, fish, cakes, biscuits, chocolate, apples, oranges and lemons? Valiant efforts were made. In 1942 the Ministry of Food published the advertisement 'Fruitful results from Vegetables', which suggested that the daily requirement of Vitamin C should be obtained by eating a 'good portion' of raw shredded sprouts, raw shredded spinach or shredded swede or turnip – 'The Vitamin C value will be increased if you use parsley or mustard and cress as a garnish', the advertisement adds encouragingly. It was also suggested that mashed parsnips flavoured with banana essence would be difficult to distinguish from the genuine article!

Dried egg powder from America was available from 1942 and a tin containing the equivalent of a dozen eggs was offered for each consumer registered for shell eggs, 'extra to your regular egg ration'. Experiments were also made with dried vegetables, but on the whole, these were so unpalatable that it took another twenty years before anyone tried to market dried vegetables commercially in England.

These children don't seem convinced that carrots on sticks are a good substitute for ice-lollies!

'The main street was by now empty: today nothing more would happen. Before noon the housewives had swarmed, so completely, whitely, stripping the shops that one might ask oneself why these remained open. A scale or two adhered to the fishmonger's marble slab; the pastrycook's glass shelves showed a range of interesting crumbs; the fruiterer filled a longstanding void with fans of cardboard bananas and a 'Dig for Victory' placard; the greengrocer's crates had been emptied of all but earth by those who had somehow failed to dig hard enough. The butcher flaunted unknown joints of purplish meat in the confidence that these could not be bought; the dairy restricted itself to a china cow; the grocer, with costless courage kept intact his stocks of dummy cartons and tins. In the confectioner's windows the ribbons bleached on dummy boxes of chocolate among flyblown cut-outs of pre-war blonds. Newsagents without newspapers gave out in angry red chalk that they had no matches either. Pasted inside a telephone booth, a notice asked one to telephone less.'

Elizabeth Bowen, *The Heat of the Day*, 1949

	On the stove	In the hay-box
Vegetable soups (dried pea, etc)	45 mins	4 hours
Potato or root vegetable soup	15 mins	1¼ hours
Plain meat stew	30 mins	3½ hours
Meat pudding (boiling)	45 mins	3 hours
Oatmeal porridge	5 mins	6 hours
Rice	2–3 mins	2½ hours
Stewed dried fruit	2–3 mins	3½ hours
Stewed fresh fruit	2–3 mins	1½ hours
Suet pudding (boiling)	30 mins	2½ hours

The population were exhorted to save fuel, as well as making the most of the ingredients available, by cooking conservatively. Porridge cooked overnight in a hay-box satisfied both these requirements and the ubiquitous Ministry of Food was quick to encourage such economies as an individual portable hay-box as a Christmas gift: 'You can make a portable hay-box from a spare gas-mask carrier. It's very simple. Full directions will be sent if

A wartime canteen where you could eat and keep fit!

you write to the Ministry of Food.' One big baking session a week and the use of a pressure-cooker were other fuel economies advocated.

Married women engaged in war work might be able to avoid the added burden of queuing for food. The government issued a priority shopping card which should have guaranteed its possessor immediate service. The demand for women workers to replace men who were in the armed forces also led to radical change in many a housewife's lifestyle. The touching advertisement which describes the quandary of the ARP Warden who couldn't give her husband a hot pudding until she discovered Mrs Peek's Puddings illustrates an acceleration of change for both the average married woman and the food industry!

Mass catering – works canteens and, later, the government-run British Restaurants – helped to supplement many people's rations. In Sheffield the Civil Restaurants, controlled by the City Council, were so successful that, in a *Daily Telegraph* news item in 1947, Councillor J Morris said that the council intended to continue as restaurateurs: 'It will be useless for private traders to squeal about it.'

'It was always a bad day when you had to go to the British Restaurant...Eating in the British Restaurant was awfully like being fed by the Government – positively by the Minister of Food himself.'

Edmund Blishen, *A Cack-handed War*, 1972

HEALTH

One, almost incidental, by-product of the necessity for both organisation and adjustment of food supplies and diet throughout the country between 1939 and 1945 was actually an overall improvement in the health of the British people. In 1939 half the people of Britain were suffering some degree of malnutrition. Although the average daily consumption of calories was 3,000 in both 1939 and 1945, great changes in distribution had been achieved. Lord Woolton's National Milk Scheme concentrated limited supplies on 'priority' adults and on children and by 1943 consumption of milk per head had tripled in some areas. The Government's Vitamin Welfare Scheme for children, which was introduced in December 1941, supplied children with cod liver oil and, later, with orange juice. The absence of imported grain coupled with the Government's determination to impose health on the population and to avoid bread rationing (which it did – until after the war) lead to the introduction of the National Loaf in 1941. This was made of home-grown flour which contained not less than

Opposite: Children enjoying an unexpected treat of cheese sandwiches

85% of the whole grain, was grey in colour and extremely unpopular with most of the people in Britain.

In 1934, the School Medical Officer for Glossop designed a free school meal to supply school children suffering from malnutrition with the constituents missing from their home food.

A baker demonstrates how to make a National Loaf

The wartime Glossop Health Sandwich consisted of:

1 pint of milk and 1 orange, when obtainable

if no fruit, ¼ oz chopped parsley is included in the sandwich filling

3 oz wholemeal bread

¾ oz butter or vitaminised margarine

¾ oz salad; mustard and cress, or watercress, or lettuce or tomato or carrot

1½ oz cheese, or salmon, or herring, or sardine or liver

³⁄₁₆ oz dried brewers' yeast

'So I will bow to dear brown bread, Because, as my wise rulers say, We shall save tonnage this way. But let this point be understood – No man can tell me it is good.'

A P Herbert

The affluent minority of the population in 1939 also actually benefited from the wartime regime. In 'It's That Meal Again', a BBC television programme shown on 31 December 1989, adults spending six weeks on a wartime diet showed a small reduction in weight and a significant drop in the level of cholesterol in their blood. As Violet Plimmer points out: 'Highly seasoned foods and drinks, sweet and stimulating, iced or unnaturally hot, gave an immediate and fictitious sense of well-being and are very popular. Many of these delights have vanished or are restricted in amount and will become ever more rare as the war goes on. Luckily they are unnecessary and their absence may toughen rather than weaken our fibre and powers of resistance. In spite of many inconveniences, we have (at the time of writing, January 1941) suffered no limitations that will undermine health if the foods that are available are suitably combined.' Back to Doctor Carrot and Potato Pete! But it's worth remembering that national malnutrition during the First World War had peaked when the potato crop failed in 1917 and that thousands died in the subsequent influenza epidemic.

DOCTOR CARROT
the Children's best friend

THE BATTLEFRONT

One section of the community was exempt from the constant need to be inventive with food. 'The food for the Army is planned to imitate the diet that was most popular in peace time for those who could afford it. Food-stuffs of animal origin appear, if possible, at three meals a day,' writes Violet Plimmer. The War Office issued a *Manual of Military Cooking and Dietary* in 1940 which amply illustrates this point: meat, tea, eggs and sugar figure as essential ingredients in soldiers' menus. 'Thousands of women aged $17\frac{1}{2}$ – 50 wanted to become cooks in the ATS and WAAF' ran the advertisements and many a hapless girl soon found herself back at school laboriously keeping her 'Progress of Work Log Book' and copying down recipes such as:

Sea pie per Hundred Men
25 lbs meat (unprepared), 50 lbs potatoes (prepared), 4 oz parsley, 6 lbs onions, 16 lbs flour, 6 lbs suet, 4 oz baking powder, 4 oz salt, water to bind

When the army was on the move at the front, ingenious devices such as the Bluff Portable Stove and the Aldershot Oven were used

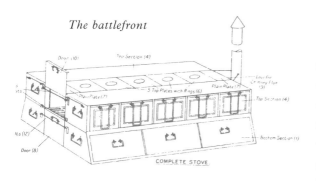

COMPLETE STOVE.

A portable stove illustrated in the *Manual of Military Cooking and Dietary*, 1940

and army catering chiefs fought with ounces of food and milligrammes of vitamins to create the one-day individual landing-rush ration in its waterproof box 15 cm x 13 cm x 5 cm (6 x 5 x 2 ins) in volume. The box contained dehydrated meat, biscuit, solid sweetened oatmeal, chocolate, tea-cubes, soup-cubes, boiled sweets and chewing gum and supplied approximately 4,000 calories.

Vitamin tablets were also supplied to supplement the soldier's diet, as the Government were very aware of the need to avoid diseases such as pellagra, beriberi and scurvy, which had been common among soldiers in all previous wars.

Unloading rations for the troops

A week's menu for the army, as dictated to an ATS recruit in 1942, compared with the spread for civilians quoted from *War at Home* by Fiona Reynoldson, and B Seebohm Rowntree's menu for a labourer in York in 1901 is shown on pp 90–1. The monotony and vitamin deficiencies in many people's diet in pre-war Britain are easily observed.

Enjoying a meal of corned beef aboard a minesweeper in the North Sea

Cocoa, more bread, or tea and a kipper or the odd slice of meat might be added as supper to the 1901 diet, while the army were served cocoa and a 'buffet' before they went to bed. On the Home Front, the meagre milk supply made cocoa and the much-advertised Ovaltine a luxury which could only be approximated with reconstructed National Dried Milk!

LUNCH

Day	1901	1942 Home Front	1942 Battle Front
Monday	Pork, potatoes, pudding, tea	Jam sandwiches	Cottage pie, mashed potatoes, cauliflower, damson pie
Tuesday	Pork, bread, tea	Potato crisp sandwiches	Meat and potato pie, cabbage, doughnuts, custard
Wednesday	Bacon and eggs, potatoes, bread, tea	Cheese sandwiches	Preserved meat fritters, chips, cabbage, baked rice pudding
Thursday	Bread, bacon, tea	Potato crisp sandwiches	Cream of lettuce soup, brown stew, mashed potatoes, green peas, pancakes
Friday	Bread, butter, toast, tea	Spam sandwiches	Potato soup, braised beef, braised rice, fondant potatoes, stewed prunes
Saturday	Bacon, potatoes, pudding, tea	Bread and cheese	Meat pie, buttered cabbage, savoury potatoes, pineapple chunks
Sunday	Pork, onions, potatoes, Yorkshire pudding	One lamb chop, carrots, potatoes, blackberry and apple pie	Roast beef, Yorkshire pudding, roast potatoes, pear flan

TEA

Day	1901	1942 Home Front	1942 Battle Front
Monday	Bread, butter, tea	Corned beef stew with soya bean dumpling, bread & peanut butter	Fish cakes, bread and butter, jam, tea
Tuesday	Bread, butter, boiled eggs, tea	Whalemeat, carrots, potatoes, suet pudding	Boiled ham, bread and butter, jam, tea
Wednesday	Bread, butter, tea	Scrambled dried eggs, stewed apples	Welsh Rarebit, bread and butter, jam, tea
Thursday	Bread, butter, tea	Baked potatoes, cake made with dried eggs	Lettuce and pies, bread and butter, jam, tea
Friday	Bread, butter, tea	Liver, one sausage, potato, bread and butter	Fish, bread and butter, jam, tea
Saturday	Bread, butter, shortcake, tea	Dried egg omelette, cabbage, potatoes, carrot flan	Pasties, bread and butter, tea
Sunday	Bread, butter, shortcake, tea	Potato pie, bread and butter, jam	Sausage rolls, lettuce, bread and butter, jam, tea

BIBLIOGRAPHY

100 Recipes for Unrationed Meat Dishes, published by Good Housekeeping. Undated.

The ABC of Cookery, His Majesty's Stationery Office (HMSO), 1945.

Bowen, Elizabeth, *The Heat of the Day*, Jonathan Cape, 1949.

Blishen, Edmund, *A Cack-handed War*, Thames & Hudson, 1972.

Braithwaite, Brian, Walsh, Noelle & Davies, Glyn (compilers), *The Home Front: The Best of Good Housekeeping 1939–1945*, Ebury Press, 1987.

Briggs, Susan, *Keep Smiling Through: The Home Front 1939-45*, Weidenfeld and Nicolson, 1975.

Food Education Memoranda from the Board of Education. *Salads and Vegetables, Good Fare in War Time; Food from Abroad*, HMSO, 1941.

Food Facts for the Kitchen Front, Collins, 1941.

Good Eating: Suggestions for Wartime Dishes, published by Hutchinson by 'reader-tested recipes' in the *Daily Telegraph*. Undated.

Good Fare, compiled by the *Daily Telegraph* Home Cook, Hutchinson. Undated.

Good Housekeeping Bulletins. Undated.

Hartley, L P, *The Go-Between*, Hamish Hamilton, 1953.

Marrack, J R, *Food and Planning*, Victor Gollancz, 1942.

Minns, Raynes, *Bombers and Mash: The Domestic Front 1939–1945*, Virago, 1980.

Macauley, Rose, *The World My Wilderness*, Collins, 1950.

Patten, Marguerite, *We'll Eat Again*, Hamlyn, 1985.

Plimmer, Violet G, *Food Values in Wartime*, Longmans & Green, 1941.

Powell, Anthony, A *Dance to the Music of Time 8: The Soldier's Art*, 1966.

Reynoldson, F, *War at Home*, Heinemann, 1980.

Skyes, L, *The "Olio" Cookery Book*, Ernest Benn, 1947.

Thirkell, Angela, *Growing Up*, Book Club, 1945.

Waller, Jane & Vaughan-Rees, Michael, *Women in Wartime: The Role of Women's Magazines 1939–1945*, Macdonald, 1987.

War Time Cookery Book, published by the *Daily Express*, November 1939.

Wartime 'Good Housekeeping' Cookery Book, compiled by the Good Housekeeping Institute, Penguin, 1942.

ACKNOWLEDGEMENTS

The publishers would like to thank the Avoncroft Museum of Historic Buildings in Bromsgrove, Worcestershire, for allowing us to use their 1940s prefab to prepare and present the recipes. We would also like to thank James O Davies and Peter Williams for their superb photography.

The author and English Heritage greatfully acknowledge the help given by Jenny Pile, Psyche Corbishley, Elizabeth Rumble, Margaret Booker, Barbara Bache, Mary Chrystal, Peggy Lord, René Rodgers and Rob Richardson.

We would also like to thank the following people and organisations listed below for permission to reproduce the photographs in this book. Every care has been taken to trace copyright holders, but any omissions will, if notified, be corrected in any future edition.

All photographs are © English Heritage or © Crown copyright.NMR with the exception of the following: Front cover Getty Images; pp 7, 9, 10, 11, 30, 31, 35, 37, 39, 43, 51, 64, 65, 66, 68, 70, 71, 72, 77, 80, 84, 86, 88, 89 by permission of the Imperial War Museum, London; p 67 Mary Evans Picture Library; pp 13, 74, 82 Getty Images; back cover Chris Hull.

RECIPE INDEX

Other titles in this series:

Prehistoric Cookery

Roman Cookery

Medieval Cookery

Tudor Cookery

Stuart Cookery

Georgian Cookery

Victorian Cookery

MINISTRY OF FOOD—Rationing Year 1953-54

4 Week Period	Week No.	RATION WEEK Sunday—Saturday	4 Week Period	Week No.	RATION WEEK Sunday—Saturday
		1953			**1953**
1	1	17 May – 23 May	7	25	1 Nov. – 7 Nov.
	2	24 May – 30 May		26	8 Nov. – 14 Nov.
	3	31 May – 6 June		27	15 Nov. – 21 Nov.
	4	7 June – 13 June		28	22 Nov. – 28 Nov.
2	5	14 June – 20 June	8	29	29 Nov. – 5 Dec.
	6	21 June – 27 June		30	6 Dec. – 12 Dec.
	7	28 June – 4 July		31	13 Dec. – 19 Dec.
	8	5 July – 11 July		32	20 Dec. – 26 Dec.
					1954
3	9	12 July – 18 July	9	33	27 Dec. – 2 Jan.
	10	19 July – 25 July		34	3 Jan. – 9 Jan.
	11	26 July – 1 Aug.		35	10 Jan. – 16 Jan.
	12	2 Aug. – 8 Aug.		36	17 Jan. – 23 Jan.
4	13	9 Aug. – 15 Aug.	10	37	24 Jan. – 30 Jan.
	14	16 Aug. – 22 Aug.		38	31 Jan. – 6 Feb.
	15	23 Aug. – 29 Aug.		39	7 Feb. – 13 Feb.
	16	30 Aug. – 5 Sept.		40	14 Feb. – 20 Feb.
5	17	6 Sept. – 12 Sept.	11	41	21 Feb. – 27 Feb.
	18	13 Sept. – 19 Sept.		42	28 Feb. – 6 Mar.
	19	20 Sept. – 26 Sept.		43	7 Mar. – 13 Mar.
	20	27 Sept. – 3 Oct.		44	14 Mar. – 20 Mar.
6	21	4 Oct. – 10 Oct.	12	45	21 Mar. – 27 Mar.
	22	11 Oct. – 17 Oct.		46	28 Mar. – 3 Apl.
	23	18 Oct. – 24 Oct.		47	4 Apl. – 10 Apl.
	24	25 Oct. – 31 Oct.		48	11 Apl. – 17 Apl.
			13	49	18 Apl. – 24 Apl.
				50	25 Apl. – 1 May
				51	2 May – 8 May
				52	9 May – 15 May

For F.O. use